Chapter One

Mum was taking Lin and Jun to the fair. "When I went last year the rides were really fun," cheered Lin.

Jun had never been to the fair before.
"Take it in turns to choose a ride," said Mum.

IT'S TOO SCARY!

ADAM & CHARLOTTE GUILLAIN

ILLUSTRATED BY SHARON DAVEY

BLOOMSBURY EDUCATION

BLOOMSBURY EDUCATION
Bloomsbury Publishing Plc
50 Bedford Square, London, WC1B 3DP, UK

BLOOMSBURY, BLOOMSBURY EDUCATION and the Diana logo are
trademarks of Bloomsbury Publishing Plc

First published in Great Britain 2019 by Bloomsbury Publishing Plc
Text copyright © Adam Guillain and Charlotte Guillain, 2019
Illustrations copyright © Sharon Davey, 2019

Adam Guillain, Charlotte Guillain and Sharon Davey have asserted their rights under the
Copyright, Designs and Patents Act, 1988, to be identified as Authors and Illustrator of this work

A catalogue record for this book is available from the British Library

ISBN: PB: 978-1-4729-6254-6; ePDF: 978-1-4729-6255-3; ePub: 978-1-4729-6253-9
enhanced ePub: 978-1-4729-6956-9

2 4 6 8 10 9 7 5 3 1

Printed and bound in China by Leo Paper Products, Heshan, Guangdong

MIX
Paper from
responsible sources
FSC® C020056

All papers used by Bloomsbury Publishing Plc are natural, recyclable products from wood
grown in well managed forests. The manufacturing processes conform to the environmental
regulations of the country of origin

To find out more about our authors and books visit www.bloomsbury.com
and sign up for our newsletters

"I'm not going on anything scary," said Jun.

The loud music made Jun's heart beat fast. "Let's ride the roller coaster!" said Lin.

"Why is everyone on it screaming?"
asked Jun, nervously.
"Because it's exciting," said Lin.
"It's too scary," said Jun.

Chapter Two

Jun chose the first game. It was called hook a duck.

"I caught a duck!" he shouted.

"Well done," said Mum, smiling.
"Only one?" said Lin. "I've got
three already."

9

Lin chose to play at the coconut shy next.
Jun found it very hard.

When Lin knocked a coconut down she won a big cuddly teddy bear.
"It's not fair!" said Jun.

Mum bought Lin and Jun some candy floss.
"Please can we ride on the roller coaster,"
Lin begged.
"It's too big," said Jun.

"Last year Lin felt just the same," said Mum, kindly.
"No, I did not!" snapped Lin.

Chapter Three

Lin really wanted to try a new ride.
"Let's go on the ghost train!" she called.

Jun stared at the strange pictures.
"It looks too spooky," he said.

Then Lin ran to a ride called the waltzer.
"Last year this ride was awesome,"
she cried.

"But the chairs are turning too fast!" said Jun.
"Well, what do you want to do?" said Lin impatiently.

Jun chose the teapot ride.
"But this is just for babies!" wailed Lin.

Then Lin stopped for a moment. She
knew she had to help Jun get over his
fear of big rides.
"I know!" she said.

Chapter Four

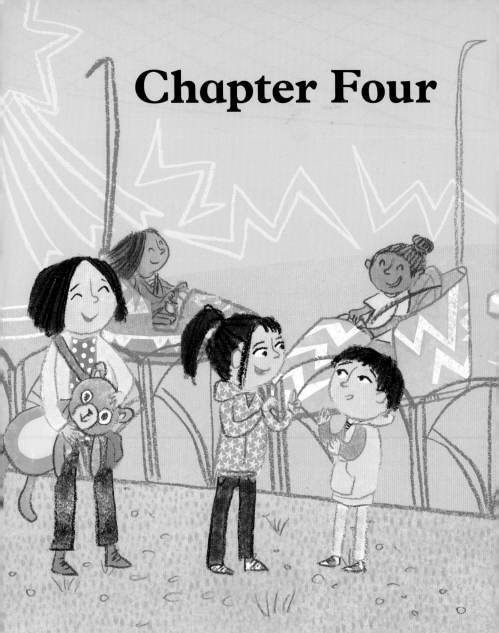

Lin stood with Jun to watch the dodgems.
"I was a bit scared of this ride last year,"
admitted Lin.

"Really?" said Jun.

"Mum helped me," said Lin. "It was fun. Shall we ride together?"

Jun loved banging and crashing
his dodgem.
"This is really fun!" he shouted.
When Jun's dodgem got stuck Lin
helped him.

After the ride was over Jun was very excited.
"I want to do more rides!" he cried.

Jun went straight back to the ghost train.
Lin and Mum were very surprised.

"That was spooky and fun!" Jun
shouted after the ride.

After that, Lin pointed at the waltzer.
This time Jun said, "Yes!"
"Ahhh!" they both screamed happily.

It was Jun's turn to choose the last ride. "It's been brilliant coming to the fair with you, Jun," said Lin.

She gave her brother her cuddly bear.
Jun beamed at her but Lin gazed sadly
up at the roller coaster.

Chapter Five

"Let's go on the roller coaster!" said Jun.
Lin could not believe Jun had chosen it.
"I feel a bit scared," said Jun as they got
in the car.

"We'll be brave together," said Lin.
When they got to the top they both gulped.

Lin and Jun screamed as they zoomed down the track.

"This ride is amazing!" yelled Lin.
"It's the best ride of all!" Jun shouted.

"Thanks Mum!" said Lin and Jun
after the fair.
"What did you like best?" said Mum.
"EVERYTHING!" cheered Lin and
Jun together.